002

003

004

005

"Ramsès" Paris

006

EAU
DE
COLOGNE
CHÈVREFEUILLE

A. PICARD
PARIS

007

SAVON
À
L'ORIGAN

LORENZY-PALANCA
PARIS

008

009

010

011

012

013

014

015

ROGER
BRODERS

GRASSE
STATION CLIMATIQUE

LA VILLE DES FLEURS ET DES PARFUMS

017

018

019

020

021

QUEEN BEAUTY

022

BACORN'S
Lilac
WITCH HAZEL
4 Fld. Ounces

Makers of Skin-Glo Creme
THE BACORN CO.
Perfumers
ELMIRA, N. Y.

023

QUEEN BEAUTY

024

N'ARD
—
THE STANDARD
PERFUMES CO.
NEW-YORK, U.S.A.

025

SALKO

Florida Water

SALUX
PERFUMER
St.Louis,
U.S.A.

026

Lady Marian
TOILET WATER

Salux
Perfumer
St.Louis,
U.S.A.

027

028

HELIOTROPE
THE STANDARD
PERFUMES CO.
NEW-YORK U.S.A.

029

7

030

031

032

033

034

FLORAL BOOKMARK

CASHMERE BOUQUET
Perfume

035

036

037

038

039

040

9

042

043

044

045

046

047

048

050

049

051

052

053

054

055

057

058

056

059

13

060

061

062

063

Savon Extra-Fin
A LA
Violette
Savonnerie du Levant
PARIS
N.º 963

065

066

EAU
DE
COLOGNE

067

068

069

070

071

072

073

17

074

075

PARFVM
ÉLÉGANT

LAURIS
SAVZÉ FRÈRES ~ PARIS

076

BACORN'S
Supreme Violet
Toilet Water
4 Fluid Ounces
Makers of
Skin-Glo
Creme

THE BACORN CO.
PERFUMERS
Elmira, N. Y.

077

=EAU=
DE
COLOGNE
AMBRÉE
MÉRIDI
PARIS

078

WHITE ROSE
LA GUILBERT
Perfumer
N.Y.

079

CARNATION
PINK
C.M. RICH
PERFUMER
N.Y.

080

Palmers
ROB ROY

ROB ROY
Palmer
New York

083

BACORN'S
CRAB APPLE
TOILET WATER
4 Fluid Ounces
Makers of Skin-Glo Creme

THE BACORN CO.
PERFUMERS
Elmira, N. Y.

082

081

084

SAN REMO

Toilet
Water
A
DELIGHTFUL
TOILET REQUISITE

Dr. J.B. Lynas & Son,
Perfumers.
LOGANSPORT,
IN D.

085

086

087

088

089

091

092

093

094

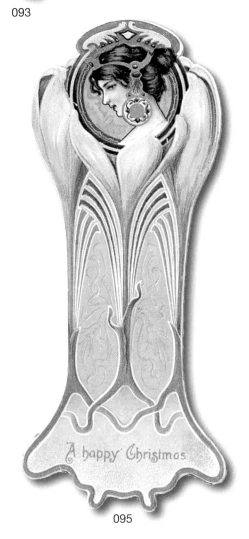

095

096

097

098

099

23

101

102

104

103

105

106

107

108

109

110

111

112

113

114

115

116

117

28

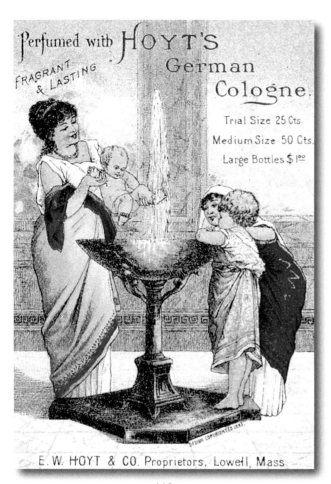

118

119

120

121

122

123

124

125

126

127

128

129

130

131

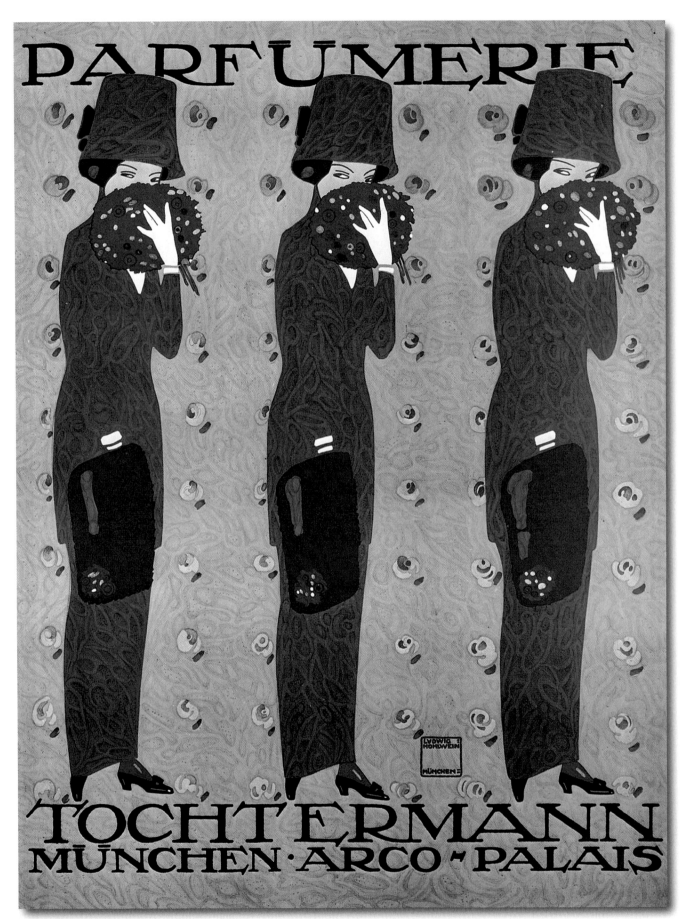

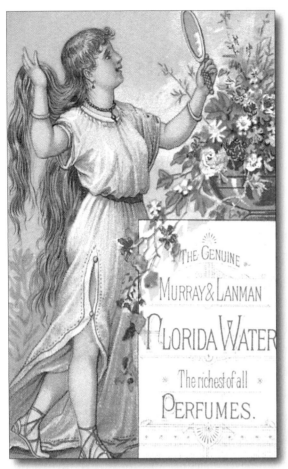

135

136

137

138

139

140

142

141

144

143

146

147

148

149

BACORN'S
Trailing Arbutus
Toilet Water
4 Fld. Ounces
Makers of Skin-Glo
Creme

The Bacorn Co.
PERFUMERS
Elmira, N. Y.

150

EAU DE
COLOGNE
SUPÉRIEURE

151

BACORN'S
Lily of
the Valley
TOILET WATER
4 Fluid Ounces
Makers of Skin-Glo
Creme

THE BACORN CO.
PERFUMERS
Elmira, N. Y.

152

CARNATION
PINK
C.M.RICH
Perfumer
N.Y.

153

LILY
OF THE VALLEY
C.M.RICH
Perfumer
N.Y.

154

EAU
DE
Cologne
Viridiflor
CHYPRE
Jⁿ Giraud. Fils
· PARIS ·

155

156

EAU
DE
Cologne
Viridiflor
MIMOSA
Jⁿ Giraud. Fils
· PARIS ·

157

38

Concerto

SUR UN THÈME
DE JASMIN

UN PARFUM
EXCLUSIVITÉ GRANDS MAGASINS DU **LOUVRE**-PARIS

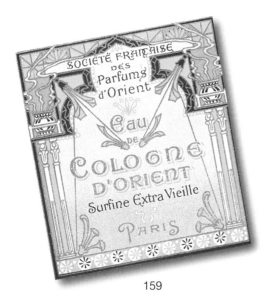

159

160

161

162

163

164

FLORIDA BREEZE"

"MARTHA WASHINGTON"

"SPANISH JESSAMINE"

"GOLDEN GATE"

"EDGEWOOD VIOLETS"

RICKSECKER'S PERFUMES.

165

IMPORTED

BAY RUM

FOR EXTERNAL USE ONLY
ALCOHOL CONTENTS 50%
BOTTLED BY
PHIL. EISEMANN
616 N. QUEEN ST.
LANCASTER, PA.

166

EAU DE COLOGNE
AUX FLEURS
AU CAPITOLE - TOULOUSE

167

LADIES CALENDAR FOR 1892

PERFUMED WITH

HOYT'S GERMAN COLOGNE

THE MOST

FRAGRANT

AND

LASTING

OF ALL

PERFUMES.

USE

RUBIFOAM

FOR

THE TEETH

Price 25 cts a Bottle.

168

LADIES' PERFUMED CALENDAR

1895

COMPLIMENTS OF

E.W. HOYT & CO.,
LOWELL, MASS.

PROPRIETORS OF

HOYT'S GERMAN COLOGNE RUBIFOAM FOR THE TEETH.

169

Standard
BAY RUM
Contains 37% Grain Alcohol.

GUARANTEED BY Phil Eisemann UNDER FOOD &
DRUG ACT, JUNE 30, 1906, SERIAL NO.
34078

Prepared by
PHIL EISEMANN
LANCASTER, PA.

170

41

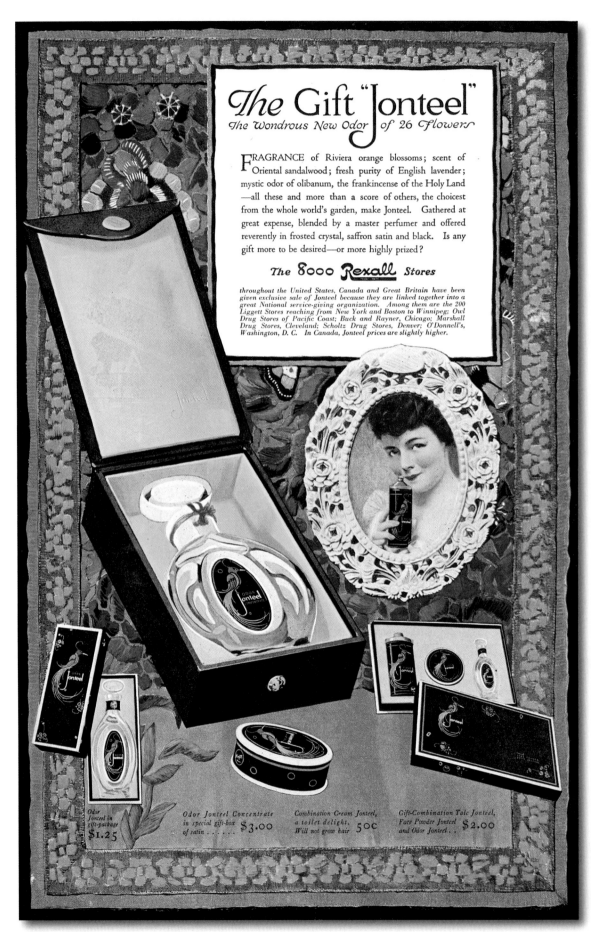

172

173

174

175

43

176

177

178

179

180

181

Fashions in Fragrance

*F*RAGRANCE is the *soul* of Fashion. It senses the inner beauty and meaning of color, line and form, stirs the emotions, expresses personality. The fragrance of the rose *is* the rose. In its fragrance it lives forever. Fashion is like its changing form and fading color. This is why the fragrant creations of the Parisian parfumeurs, Roger & Gallet, have played so distinctive and lasting a part in the fashions of three generations.

"Fashions in Fragrance" is the title of a fragrant, colorful, little, 64 page booklet just issued. It is the why and how, the when and where, in the use of Fragrance—the story of fifty years of fashions in fragrance as Fashion has expressed itself in its preference for Roger & Gallet products. Mailed free on request of Roger & Gallet, 25 West 32nd Street, New York.

ROGER & GALLET
PARFUMEURS
PARIS NEW YORK

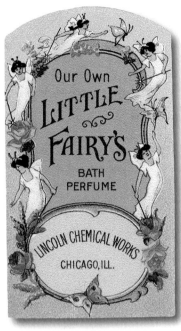

Our Own
LITTLE
FAIRY'S
BATH
PERFUME

LINCOLN CHEMICAL WORKS
CHICAGO, ILL.

183

184

ROYAL BOUQUET
FACE
LOTION
TOILET WATER

TRADE
MARK

AN EXCELLENT
TOILET PREPARATION
DELIGHTFUL LASTING
REFRESHING
INVALUABLE AFTER SHAVING

PREPARED BY
V. J. CURCIO CO.
CHEMISTS & PERFUMERS
JERSEY CITY, N.J.

185

VIOLET
LA GUILBERT
Perfumer
N.Y.

186

NARCISSUS

187

HELIOTROPE
C. M. RICH
Perfumer
N.Y.

188

SUPERIOR

COLOGNE

189

VIOLET PERFUMED

STANDARD AMERICAN

FOR
TOILET
USES

TRADE MARK

DIAMOND
EXTRACT
OF
WITCH-HAZEL

MANUFACTURED BY WM. J. UEBLER, FRANKFORT, N.Y.

190

BUERGER'S
Bonnie
Lassie
Spicy

a New and Delightful
Toilet Essential

THE BUERGER BROS.
SUPPLY CO.
DENVER

191

192

193

194

195

47

The Seven Wise Women of Persia

in an ancient book —
advise young women:

"If you meet a handsome young man in the way, cunningly remove a little of the veil and draw it off gradually, pretending—'It is very hot, how I perspire, my heart is wounded.' Talk on in this manner and stand a little until the youth looking captivated smells the perfume of Ottar and sends a message describing his enchanted and bewildered state of mind."

It is still customary the world over to move the veil (as if by accident), but Youth is no longer captivated by the perfume of the simple Ottar; to-day the ladies of Persia, like those of France and America, have adopted

Mary Garden Perfume

that remarkable medium of personal expression
created by

Rigaud

Master Perfumer of Paris
19 Rue de la Paix, Paris
and New York

Mary Garden Perfume, Toilet Water, Sachet, Talcum and Face Powders, Rouge, (Vanity Case), Massage, Cold and Greaseless Creams, Soap and Breath Tablets.

From a drop of Mary Garden Perfume radiates an ocean of influence.

Lilas de Rigaud —the only odor true to the fresh Lilac flower